The Real Story
The Confessio
The Antipriest

By: Yves Dupont

Table of Contents

Introduction

In 1972 Yves Dupont published the <u>Story of Seminary Student 1025</u>, which details a true story of Communist infiltration into the Catholic Church. About the same time TAN Books published a fictionalized version of this work as <u>AA-1025</u>. This work is quite popular, but useless in presenting the case for what may have happened in the 1960's to the Catholic Church.

The important point is that this is a true story written by the conspirator himself. It was discovered, when he was in a car accident. He had kept a diary of his perfidious dealings as an Anti-Apostle.

But this is not the only proof that The Enemy, the Devil, has been guiding people to infiltrate the Catholic Church. Pope Saint Pius X warned in <u>Pascendi</u>:

> That We make no delay in this matter is rendered necessary especially by the fact that the partisans of error are to be sought not only among the Church's open enemies; they lie hid, a thing to be deeply deplored and feared, in her very bosom and heart, and are the more mischievous, the less conspicuously they appear. We allude, Venerable Brethren, to many who belong to the Catholic laity, nay, and this is far more lamentable, to the ranks of the priesthood itself, who, feigning a love for the Church, lacking the firm protection of philosophy and theology, nay more, thoroughly imbued with the poisonous doctrines taught by the enemies of the Church, and lost to all sense of modesty, vaunt themselves as reformers of the Church; and, forming more boldly into line of attack, assail all that is most sacred in the work of Christ, not sparing even the person of the Divine Redeemer, whom, with sacrilegious daring, they reduce to a simple, mere man.

Pope Pius IX earlier had the <u>Permanent Instruction of the Alta Vendita</u> delivered to him. He ordered it published, as it detailed the Masonic plan to infiltrate the Catholic Church in order to destroy it. This is reproduced here as well as another short item on a third group working to infiltrate the Catholic Church.

We must remember that the Devil hates the Catholic Church and his sole desire is to destroy it so that more souls will damn themselves to eternal misery with him in Hell. We must remember that the Devil is our real enemy. Men may work with the Devil, but the Devil is the real enemy behind these conspiracies.

The Confession Of Mikolaj
The Antipriest

This man has no name, but we shall call him Mikolaj because he came from Poland where he was born in 1917, perhaps from Russian parents fleeing the Revolution. He was found wandering along a road at the age of three, by a Polish Doctor and his wife, both devout Catholics. The year of his birth must have been determined by the Doctor because the child, who was crying, spoke only a little Polish and a little Russian and did not even know his own name. The Polish couple had no child of their own. They adopted him and loved him as their own son. In his confession, Mikolaj related that his foster parents were very good to him, very generous, full of affection, and that this recollection, even fifty years later, filled him with "seething Anger". For he had been trained, as an agent of the devil, to hate what normal people respect and love. Memories of his childhood were like intruders trying to move his heart and bring about his conversion. He could not bear them, he had to hate them, and hate also those who were responsible for these sweet memories. The child grew into a boy of quiet disposition and studious habits. His intelligence and capacity for learning appear to have been extraordinary, and so was his ambition. The latter seems to have played an important part in his downfall at the age of 14 or 15 when, one evening, shortly before a planned visit to Rome and Paris, he overheard his parents express their concern about his passport and his legal status as an adopted child. He was shattered! He had been brought up to believe that these two were really Mother and Father to him, and to discover this was not the truth was a great shock to him. He could not get over it. They died in his heart as effectively as if they had died physically. They ceased to be "Mum and Dad". They became "Those People". Distracted almost out of his mind, he fled from the house immediately. He decided to leave Poland, and made for the Russian border. A schoolmate of his had an uncle in Russia, in Leningrad to be precise, where he was as a high ranking public servant. A few days later, with a letter of introduction in his hand, he called at the uncle's home in Russia. The uncle noticed his alertness, intelligence and ambition, and was favorably impressed.

"If you wish to succeed, my lad," he told him, "first of all you must study some foreign languages and absorb the doctrine of the Party."

For the next six years, Mikolaj studied furiously and absorbed the Marxist doctrine in its entirety. The uncle, as he soon found out, was a high ranking official in the Secret Police. There is little doubt that his interest for the young man had been aroused by considerations which had little to do with affection or sympathy. The boy was highly intelligent, had no parents or relative to divide his allegiance or interfere with his Marxist studies, and he was ambitious. In fact, the perfect raw material with which to form a good agent. Other factors, too, contributed to this. Mikolaj had an enormous capacity for work, a remarkable memory, and he despised all women and the "fools" who love them too much. This would exclude emotional involvements with the fair sex.

The six years of study completed, Mikolaj, now 20, was called to the office of the Uncle who told him point blank:

"I am going to send you abroad to become a militant atheist on the world scene. Your main duty will be to fight all religions, but the Catholic religion in particular because of its efficient structures. In order to achieve this you will enter a seminary and become a Catholic priest. But you must return to Poland and seek reconciliation with your foster parents who will be delighted to hear of your "vocation" and who will help you to become a priest."

Mikolaj had mixed feelings. The idea of being a secret agent filled him with elation, but the command to see his "parents" again and act the part of a loving son for the six long years which he would spend in the seminary, was abhorrent to him. Self control is one of the qualities of a secret agent. In this case, however, Mikolaj could not quite conceal his feelings even after 6 years of training in Marxist schools. The Uncle remarked on this, which had Mikolaj blush, and drew a further remark from the Uncle:

"A secret agent does not blush, has no blood in his veins, has no heart, loves no one not even himself. He is the Thing of the Party, and the Party can devour him alive and without warning. Wherever you are, get it into your head that you will be watched. At the first sign of weakness we shall get rid of you. And, of course, if you are in danger, do not rely on us. You will be disavowed."

Answered Mikolaj: "I know all this very well, but I beg to ask why I should show love and affection to my false parents when I feel nothing but hatred for them."

"Hatred has no room in our service, except the hatred of God following Lenin's example. We kill without hatred simply to serve the Party. You must see your parents again, but you will not enter a Polish seminary. You will be sent overseas, perhaps to Canada, where discipline is not as strict as in Europe, and there is less likelihood of discovery. Besides, with that madman now in Germany we have every reason to fear a war in Europe."

The Uncle gave him further instructions and reminders: "Persecution is useless. We don't want any martyrs as long as we are not in complete control of the West. Religion must be destroyed by dialectics. [Dialectic: The art or practice of examining statements logically as by question and answer.] You are to send me a report every week. After a while you will be put in touch with the rest of the network and you will be responsible for ten other agents, but you will not know who they are, and they will not know you. To reach them and to reach you everything will go through this office. We already have many priests in those countries which are afflicted with Catholicism, one is a bishop. We have observers everywhere. Some, especially trained for the purpose, scan the newspapers of the whole world every day and send us reports on the development of ideas in the West. Our foreign policy is based on these. Thus we will be able to see how effective your own work is. You will have to spread new ideas. Ideas that may appeal to some stupid pen pusher who will take them up and publicize them. **No one is more vain than a writer.** Give him an idea, and he will say that it is his own, write about it, enlarge upon it, and thus further our aims. We rely a great deal on writers and journalists. There is no need for us to train them, they work for us without realizing it. You will receive letters from us. You will recognize every letter as genuine by the code numbers SS 1025, which is your own. SS means Seminary Student. **Yes, there are 1024 others.**"

The next few days Mikolaj spent most of his time studying a few confidential files the Uncle had given him. Before he left Russia, a number of further interviews with the Uncle took place. During one of these he told the Uncle of his own ideas on how best to combat religion in the West. An open and bitter opposition had already been ruled out.

Persuasion through dialectics, lectures, debates, dialogues and colloquies was the latest method favored by Moscow, and it was to develop considerably after World War II. In almost all such talks the Communist speakers, who were highly trained dialecticians, outsmarted their opponents and often silenced them completely, thus winning many "converts" in the audience. Press reports of such talks further helped to spread Marxist ideas and lent respectability to the Communists who, it was thought, had become "reasonable". The method has indeed proved extremely successful. The penetration of Marxist thinking in the West is now so thorough that echoes of it are quite a common occurrence even in the Catholic press. To complement this method, however, **Mikolaj had devised a more sinister scheme primarily designed to change Catholic doctrine**. Briefly, instead of combating the religious feeling of the people, it consisted in exalting it in a wrong direction and towards some unrealistic objective. The Uncle who, at first had seemed somewhat amused, now listened with great interest (decidedly, he thought, this young man is above average).

Mikolaj went on: "We must put it into their heads, and especially priests, that the time has come to seek and **work for the merging of all religions**. We must, in particular, promote among Catholics a feeling of guilt concerning the "One Truth" which they claim they alone possess. We must convince them that this attitude is a monstrous sin of pride, and that they must now seek reconciliation with other religions. This thought must be made to grow and be uppermost in their minds."

Answered the Uncle: "Very well! But don't you think that this scheme is somewhat unrealistic?"

"Not at all!" said Mikolaj, "I myself was a Catholic up to the age of 15, and a very devout one at that. I think it should be comparatively easy to convince Catholics that there are holy persons among Protestants, Mussulmans [Muslims] and Jews. And since they are holy, they also are the members of the "Communion of Saints" in which Catholics believe. Starting from this, we will say that to keep these people out of the Church is an insult to God. Of course, we shall drop the term "Communion of Saints". We shall substitute for it some other expression such as "Community of Believers" or "People of God". **This will shift the accent from the supernatural to the natural, from the heavenly to the earthly, which is what we want. The whole**

Catholic terminology can and must be changed. To those who object we shall reply that the meaning has not changed and that we must adapt our expressions to the modern way of thinking, which is what progress is about. And since Catholic intellectuals, like most intellectuals, seek and value the praise of others, they will be mortally afraid of being "behind the times". they will accept the new terms and promote them among the ignorant people. There is a whole area to be investigated here. I can do no more than outline the plan."

"And how do you envision that Universal Church to which you would have everyone rushing in to?"

"That new Church must be simple. The concept of God must be vague, general and impersonal, not entailing any definite obligations, not demanding sacrifices, and, of course, not providing any inspiration to the people. The universal brotherhood of men must be emphasized above all things. It should not be difficult to persuade Catholics that the Commandment "Love they neighbor as thyself" requires no less than that. In order to make them forget God, **we must get them to worship the human race.** This, however, is a long term effort: it may take 20, 30, or even 50 years.[1] We must be prepared to wait, but I am confident that we shall succeed."

"Very well, we shall examine your idea. Come back next week and we shall give you our reply. Meanwhile, get ready for your departure for Poland".

The following week Mikolaj called at the Uncle's office as arranged. The Uncle told him that his Chief was here and wanted to meet him. Mikolaj was overjoyed, for it was obvious that such a powerful Official would not come merely to signify his refusal. He must have been favorably impressed. Completely self possessed, Mikolaj met the great Chief. However, he instantly disliked his appearance which was one of gross brutality and vulgarity. He reflected that this must be the sort of man who enjoys watching the most cruel tortures in prisons: a true sadist. Mikolaj was above all an intellectual. He disliked the idea of torture which he saw as a mark of weakness and stupidity on the part of the torturer. The Chief looked at him in a manner that

---

[1]   1937 + 20 years = 1957
        1937 + 30 years = 1967
        1937 + 50 years = 1987

11

bore right through him. Mikolaj felt uneasy. Point blank, the Chief asked: "What do you have most at heart?"

"The victory of the Party," said Mikolaj.

"Good! From today onwards you will be on the roll of our active agents. You will have responsibilities, you will issue orders. But make no mistake about it. We expect to see the fruits of your work in newspapers, books and theological reviews. It is up to you. We have a specialist team of readers whose function it is to analyze the religious writings of the whole world. We will watch your progress. However, I am confident that you will be able to handle this."

Mikolaj reflected that this brute, after all, was no fool. He had correctly assessed his exceptional ability and his outstanding intelligence of which he never doubted himself. He felt completely sure that he would succeed, for he knew well the weak spot of Catholics, which is Charity. With "Charity" it is always possible to instill remorse in the hearts of people, and a remorseful person is inevitably in a state of lesser resistance and, therefore, of higher receptivity to alien ideas and suggestions. This is psychologically certain, just as certain as pure mathematics. With "Charity" it will be possible to persuade Catholics it is a sin to criticize Protestants, Jews, and Mussulmans [Muslims], and that to criticize their beliefs is, in fact, the same as criticizing them. **Thus, Catholics will gradually accept the beliefs of the other religions and their own faith will wane.** The honesty and scruples of Catholics, Mikolaj thought, is the opening through which we shall enter their fortress. It is the fault in the rock that can be plugged with explosives, the weakness which makes a dialogue with them extremely rewarding. A few days later, Mikolaj was back in Poland. He somewhat dreaded his first meeting with his foster father, so he arranged to come "home" when the Doctor was likely to be out. He rang the door bell, and it was his foster mother who came and opened the door. Here is the account of his return:

"She had aged considerably, she did not have any makeup on. She looked ill. She began to shake with emotion, then she cried. Really, women are no good except locked up in harems for the convenience of men in their necessities. Naturally, I begged her to pardon me. That was part of the game. But I knew that this business would be promptly settled, so overcome with joy would she be. Thus, I would not have to abase myself before my foster father when he came home. To see me as a priest of God must have been her most cherished dream. So, without any more ado, I told her of my "irresistible" vocation. The old goose was so happy that she nearly fainted. From then on she would have believed anything I said. And when was I for the first time aware of the "call of God"? Well, I said, it all came suddenly through an apparition. (I had not intended to tell her anything like that, but the idea came to me there and then. I knew this sort of thing would appeal to her, and it amused me anyway). Of course, the Doctor was rather suspicious of the supernatural, but that did not matter, on the contrary, any disagreement between the two could only strengthen my own position, and while they were arguing how my vocation came about, **it would not occur to them that I may not have had any vocation at all**. So I told her in great detail my story of that wonderful heavenly visitation. I said St. Anthony of Padua had come to me, and, to make the picture even nicer, I added that he was carrying the Infant Jesus in his arms. The silly old cow was near to ecstasy. Just then, however, the Doctor arrived and I was relieved to be able to speak to a sensible person after all that nonsense, but I saw immediately that he would have nothing of my story. Never mind! That will make the game even more exciting. The next day we went to see the bishop. He was kind, but reserved. That was just what I had expected. I knew very well that he would not send me to the seminary the next day! My perseverance would prove that my vocation was genuine. Throughout the interview I assumed an air of perfect humility with my eyes cast down except when I was spoken to. He advised me to go and see a Religious Priest who was known for his ability to "discern the spirits". This jargon means that the fellow was supposed to read people's hearts! So I went to see him. Our interview was a protracted one, and I did not like the character. He spoke slowly, deliberately and his speech was punctuated with long, heavy pauses that were rather unpleasant. Of course, I said nothing of my "apparitions". My mother would have most certainly told him already, and my reserve in this respect would look very edifying indeed. I played the part of a very humble young man, and I am sure that I played it most excellently. However, I took some pride in confessing to him that I had never known any girl or woman, and that I was not at all interested in the weaker sex which, in my opinion, has no other function than that of childbearing. I felt sure that he would condone such an outburst of juvenile pride, and it would show him how earnest I was. The "holy" man, however, set a few traps for me. He tried to pin me down on some contradictions. How childish! I was fully trained for that sort of thing. He also asked me why I left my foster parents six years earlier, and why I had never written to them. I thought it would be best not to attempt to justify my past behavior. On the contrary, an admission of human weakness was more likely to move his heart. So I told him in quavering tones that this folly of mine would be the remorse of my whole life. But, I added, the immense sorrow which I caused to my "dear" mother would be more than repaid by the lasting bliss of my priestly vocation, for nothing could make her more happy than that. He agreed, and I now felt certain that he would not have the heart to deprive my aging mother of such great happiness. Our conversation grew more and more friendly as the hours went by, and, when we parted, we were like two old friends. Because of this I was thunderstruck when, a few days later, the bishop told me quietly that, in this priest's opinion, I did not have a vocation. **It was as though the earth had split under my very feet.** I reported the setback to the Uncle through a priest agent who had been appointed to that function. The reply came promptly and it was a terse one:

"Destroy the obstacle."

After pondering a few days on the best way to "destroy the obstacle", a task which I did not relish, I decided to put to good use the special training in bare hand combat which I had received in Russia. But it would be better if this took place outside the priest's monastery. I arranged through my comrade the priest agent that he should invite the Religious to his home. And so it was done. I had felt humiliated and angry at having been rejected by the old coot, and when our second interview took place, I demanded to know his reasons. He calmly answered that he did not have any reason himself, but that the Lord had given him the "discerning of spirits" (I Cor.12:10). I could see that the man was not pretending, he really believed what he said, but his wholly unscientific reason did not satisfy me. How can you argue with a man who believes in magic? **Even his seraphic smile irritated me. That old man behaved like a child.** I told him that I would not hesitate to kill him if this could help me to enter the seminary. **He answered quietly that he knew this.** I was flabbergasted! For a long moment we looked at each other without saying a word. Then he broke the heavy silence and said slowly:

"You know not what you are doing."

"I must confess that I felt then extremely uncomfortable. **This man could read my mind. He possessed powers which I did not understand.** My comrade the priest, who was in the room, sensed that I was faltering. He signaled to me discreetly. In a flash I realized that I was finished unless I carried out the Uncle's orders there and then. I sprang to my feet and with two neat karate blows I killed the old man. In 1938, very few people in the West knew the possibilities afforded by this Japanese art, and I was grateful to my Russian masters for teaching me how to kill "cleanly". Those two blows had caused his heart to stop, and his death would be normally diagnosed as a heart failure. The next day, however, I had a rash all over my body, a symptom of emotional stress. How stupid of me! I was fully confident now that I would eventually enter the seminary, and I was already making plans for the future especially as regard my work for the Party. **I was to inject into Catholic thinking a whole set of new values and a new train of thought.** I was to foster remorse in their hearts, a gnawing sense of guilt, quoting the Gospel: "Be One as the Father and I are One." That sense of guilt must grow into an obsession to the point of rehabilitating Martin Luther. They will be made to believe that schisms and heresies were caused by their own intransigence, that the time had come for them to atone and make reparation by throwing their arms open to their Protestant brethren and confessing their own sin of pride and stubbornness. Of course, we shall not tamper with the Creed except for the word "Catholic" which must be changed to "Universal" or "Christian" as the Protestants use. But we shall not use the name of God except when necessary. We shall speak of man, stress his dignity and nobility. **We must transform the language and thinking pattern of every Catholic.** We must foster the mystique of the human race. At first, we shall say that God exits, but we shall point out that God remains forever outside the field of human experience, and experience is what counts for sensate beings. We shall lay much stress on experience and sensory perceptions. The positive, the experimental and the sensorial must be the basis of the new thinking. We shall say that, since God is invisible, the best way to serve Him is to set up a universal Church in which all men can meet as brothers in mutual goodwill, love, and understanding. This new mystique must finally obfuscate the concept of God of whom we shall speak less and less,

15

except for saying that we are God because God is in everyone of us. In this manner, we shall redirect the religious yearnings and superstitions of the people. We shall deify Man. Once Catholics have accepted this new mystique, we shall tell them to strip their churches bare of statues and ornaments because these things are unessential and abhorrent to their dear Protestant and Jewish brethren. Thus all symbols of Catholic worship and devotion will go by the boards, and when they are gone devotions will go too. Yes, we shall promote an iconoclastic zeal especially among the younger generation. They themselves will destroy that jumble of statues, pictures, vestments, reliquaries, organs, etc. It would be a good idea, too, to spread a "prophecy" that says:

"You shall see married priests, and **you shall hear the Mass in the language of the people."**

This should make our task easier. **We shall incite women to assert their right to the priesthood,** and we shall make the Mass more popular by allowing home Masses that can be said by the father or the mother of the family. Once this practice is established we shall campaign for the abolition of the parish system as antiquated and not in keeping with the needs of modern times. Churches can then be turned into museums, meeting halls, theaters, storerooms and other useful functions. All sorts of exciting ideas came surging into my head, and I coded my whole program before sending it to Moscow. Looking back on these days, I now feel a legitimate pride at having been the first to suggest these ideas to the Party. It is now plain that these were the right ideas, far superior to a mere dialectical attempt at destroying religious belief. Some time later, an order came from Moscow:

"New assignment: go to Rome."

And so I left Poland for what was going to be my lifetime work. Once in Rome I met a priest professor who was in our network. He was a scholar and a scriptural expert. He was then busy preparing a new English version of the Bible, but his work was still secret. In that new version the old cliches about the Virginity of Mary, the Real Presence and like fables were to be adroitly amended and reinterpreted. Instead of "Virgin" Mary will be called "maid". The "brethren" of Jesus will become His "brothers". The "Real Presence" will be explained as a feeling, or experience, when "Christians are gathered together in His name". The notion of "gathering" is an important one to promote the community spirit. Those who do not conform to the Group will be reproved as trouble makers and bad Christians. We must absolutely stifle individual attitudes if we are to control the Group as we please, and the control of the Group is essential for the establishment of Communism. The professor also taught me a sensible way to say Mass since, within six years, I shall be obliged willy nilly to say it also. He never actually pronounced the words of the Consecration. He simply muttered some words that sounded like it. This was possible since the Rubrics require that the words be said in a low voice. Later, of course, the Mass will be radically modified. We shall play down the sacrificial aspect, we shall exalt it as a meal taken by the Community. In case some reactionary priests refuse to conform, and insist on saying the old prayers, we shall direct that the Canon in its entirety be said aloud. This will also make it possible for the people to say the words with the priests, and once this is possible we shall rule that it is indispensable also. Thus the Mass will cease to be the privilege of the priest alone. **The professor was already working on a draft for a New Order of the Mass, and he urged me to do likewise because, he said, it was greatly desirable that we should give the people different kinds of Masses. This will help destroy unity, the mainstay of Catholic power. All this would be a great deal easier if we succeeded in having one of our agents elected as pope.** Failing this, however, we would probably be able to sway the Cardinals sufficiently to obtain the election of a progressive pope who will ratify whatever our agents put on his desk in the name of progress. I was fascinated by the things the professor told me, and I tried to elicit from him the names of some of the other priests and seminarians who were members of our network, but he said he knew little about it. He did say, however, that we had a few professors teaching in the Roman seminaries, and he gave me the name of another professor, a Frenchman, who was giving singing lessons in Rome. He was a member of the Communist Party, and I was told that I could trust him completely. I later met him and befriended him. One day, as we were strolling through the streets of Rome, he said:

"Imagine this city without a cassock in sight. How wonderful it would be!"

"Yes," I nodded, "the cassock must go. After all, they could say Mass in a jacket or jumper!"

"From my Catholic upbringing I understood how vocations often assert themselves in young children: in his cassock, the priest stands out as a man different from the rest. The child likes him and wants to emulate him. But destroy the cassock, and you will destroy the priest. In this way many vocations will die in the bud."

"The merging of all religions," continues Mikolaj in his confessions, "and the brotherhood of man, must always be reasserted as the basic motivation for all the changes. "Love thy neighbor as thyself" will be our scriptural justification. **The greatest change, and the most desirable one, is the suppression of the papacy**, but this appeared very difficult to me in view of Christ's promise: "Thou art the Rock, and upon this Rock I shall build My Church". **We shall therefore endeavor to undermine the authority of the pope in every possible way,** and we shall try to enlist his (the pope's) cooperation to introduce the changes that will make this possible. We shall promote the concept of Episcopal Equality and the priesthood of the laity. When the bishops are elected by the people, and the pope is no more than the president of the bishops, our victory will be near at hand. When, moreover, the parish system has been destroyed through the proliferation of home Masses celebrated **by lay folk in their capacity as "priests", the Mass itself will cease to be.** When, finally, the bishops elected by the people are admitted to vote in a conclave, then the papacy will be in our hands. All must be done in the name of love. Also in the name of love, we shall promote the idea that God is far too loving to want His only Son to die a cruel death for us and to want to create an everlasting hell. Christ will be described as a good man and great revolutionary, and hell as a superstition of the Dark Ages. **We shall no longer mention sin**, and Angels will be relegated to the realm of mythology and fairy tales. Once the people cease to fear God, they will soon forget Him. Our task is to promote these ideas among the Catholic elite via the theological journals which we control, and they in turn will promote them in the Church as their own ideas. **We shall also encourage many new translations of the Bible. The greater the number of translations, the better. It will help to create confusion.** The number of Catholic scholars who are itching to produce their own versions - undoubtedly the best ever produced in their own eyes - is not lacking. All they need is a little prodding from us. We are faced with a huge task. Many problems remain to be solved: the Rosary, Lourdes, and the twenty odd feasts of Mary are annoying things, but we shall be patient. In any case, we will have to draw up a new calendar and dispose of many Marian feasts as well as many other Saints. The new calendar must look as bare as the table on which **they will say the new Mass**. Such is the substance of the orders which I issued to the network. **The following year I began to work on the draft of a new catechism which would be acceptable to all believers**. It must be practical, human, non committal, and ambiguous. It must stress the humanity of Christ who, in fact, was a brother of ours. But the word "charity" is to be banished absolutely. We shall say "love" instead. Love can be many things, but charity has an intolerable religious connotation. We shall say, of course, that it means the same and the change is more conformable to modern usage. Concerning the precepts of the Church, we shall say that Christians are now fully mature and adult, that the precepts were necessary when the people were ignorant and uneducated, but that it is more fitting to adult Christians to let their own consciences decide. **God, in any case, is far too great and remote to worry about our eating meat on Fridays!** Private confession is a waste of time. We shall promote a communal penitential rite with emphasis on sins committed against our brothers. **The precept of Sunday attendance will be modified too.** We shall say that, because of the working conditions in this modern age, people need their Sunday to relax in the countryside away from the city's fumes. **They should be allowed to attend Mass on Saturday, even on Friday.** God did not say what day was to be reserved. In all cases we shall stress the primacy of the individual conscience over set rules and petty precepts which are unworthy of an adult man and an insult to his dignity. We shall retain the "Our Father" for the time being, but we shall replace "Thee" by "You" and we shall find suitable substitutes for such words as "forgive, temptations, trespasses" and other similar nonsense. The seven sacraments will receive our special attention. The first I would like to abolish is baptism, but it will have to stay for a while. We shall say that Original Sin is not the sin of Adam and Eve who, in any case, never existed. We shall reinterpret it. Baptism, then, will merely be a ceremony marking the coming of a new member into the human brotherhood. We shall do likewise with every Sacrament. Concerning marriage, it shall not be refused to those priests who wish to receive it. In the Mass, the words "Real Presence" and "Transubstantiation" must be deleted. We shall speak of "Meal" and "Eucharist" instead. We shall destroy the Offertory and play down the Consecration and, at the same time, we shall stress the part played by the people. In the Mass, as it is today, the priest turns his back to the people and fills a sacrificial function which is intolerable. He appears to offer his Mass to the great Crucifix hanging over the ornate altar. **We shall pull down the Crucifix, substitute a table for the altar, and turn it around so that the priest may assume a presidential function**. The priest will speak to the people much more than before. To achieve this, we shall shorten what is now called the Mass proper, and we shall add many readings to what is called the Foremass. **In this manner the Mass will gradually cease to be regarded as an act of adoration to God, and will become a gathering and an act of human brotherhood.** All these points will have to be elaborated in great detail and they may take anything up to 30 years before they are implemented, but I think that all my objectives will be fulfilled by 1974. Thus I labored for twenty long years. Pius XII died in 1958. When John XXIII announced a new council, my interest was greatly stimulated. **I reported to my chiefs that this was perhaps the last battle: no effort should be spared**. They were obviously of the same opinion because they immediately appointed me to the highest position in the West European network, and they gave me unlimited financial backing through our Bank in Switzerland. Hearing that Pope John had appointed a commission to draw the schemas of the forthcoming Council, I immediately started to work on counter schemas with the help of avant garde theologians who had been won over to our way of thinking. Thanks to my contacts I managed to obtain copies of the projected papal schemas. They were terrible! I was in a cold sweat! If these schemas are carried, my work of 20 years will have been in vain. I hastily put the finishing touch to my counter schemas, and I circulated them. Eventually, they were tabled in the Council. Thanks to the cooperation of some bishops whose thinking had been conditioned previously, the majority of bishops, reactionary but ill prepared, were completely disconcerted by the highly efficient and coherent interventions of our friends. Most of my counter schemas were carried. But I am not satisfied: many of my schemas, although they were accepted, have been watered down by Pope Paul himself in contempt of the majority vote at the Council. Fortunately, the revised versions contain many ambiguities. **In this manner, it will be possible to initiate further changes, alleging that they are in the spirit of the Council**. At any rate, Pope Paul is a progressive and a humanist. It should not be difficult to manipulate him and obtain sweeping changes in the near future. However, we must begin to work for Vatican III even now. Vatican III, as I see it, will mean the destruction of the Church and the death of God. **Then, I shall come forward, not to nail Christ upon His Cross, but God Himself into His coffin.**"

PERMANENT INSTRUCTION OF THE ALTA VENDITA

Ever since we have established ourselves as a body of action, and that order has commenced to reign in the bosom of the most distant lodge, as in that one nearest the centre of action, there is one thought which has profoundly occupied the men who aspire to universal regeneration. That is the thought of the enfranchisement of Italy, from which must one day come the enfranchisement of the entire world, the fraternal republic, and the harmony of humanity. That thought has not yet been seized upon by our brethren beyond the Alps. They believe that revolutionary Italy can only conspire in the shade, deal some strokes of the poinard to sbirri and traitors, and tranquilly undergo the yoke of events which take place beyond the Alps for Italy, but without Italy. This error has been fatal to us on many occasions. It is not necessary to combat it with phrases which would be only to propagate it. It is necessary to kill it by facts. Thus, amidst the cares which have the privilege of agitating the minds of the most vigorous of our lodges, there is one which we ought never forget.

The Papacy has at all times exercised a decisive action upon the affairs of Italy. By the hands, by the voices, by the pens, by the hearts of its innumerable bishops, priests, monks, nuns, and people in all latitudes, the Papacy finds devotedness without end ready for martyrdom, and that to enthusiasm. Everywhere, whenever it pleases to call upon them, it has friends ready to die or lose all for its cause. This is an immense leverage which the Popes alone have been able to appreciate to its full power, and as yet they have used it only to a certain extent. Today there is no question of reconstituting for ourselves that power, the prestige of which is for the moment weakened. Our final end is that of Voltaire and of the French Revolution, the destruction for ever of Catholicism and even of the Christian idea which, if left standing on the ruins of Rome, would be the resuscitation of " Christianity later on. But to attain more certainly that result, and not prepare ourselves with gaiety of heart for reverses which adjourn indefinitely, or compromise for ages, the success of a good cause, we must not pay attention to those braggarts of Frenchmen, those cloudy Germans, those melancholy Englishmen, all of whom imagine they can kill Catholicism, now with an impure song, then with an illogical deduction; at another time, with a sarcasm smuggled in like the cottons of Great Britain. Catholicism has a life much more tenacious than that. It has seen the most implacable, the most terrible adversaries; and it has often had the malignant pleasure of throwing holy water on the tombs of the most enraged. Let us permit, then, our brethren of these countries to give themselves up to the sterile intemperance of their anti-Catholic zeal. Let them even mock at our Madonnas and our apparent devotion. With this passport we can conspire at our ease, and arrive little by little at the end we have in view.

Now the Papacy has been for seventeen centuries inherent to the history of Italy. Italy cannot breathe or move without the permission of the Supreme Pastor. With him she has the hundred arms of Briareus, without him she is condemned to a pitiable impotence. She has nothing but divisions to foment, hatreds to break out, and hostilities to manifest themselves from the highest chain of the Alps to the lowest of the Appenines. We cannot desire such a state of things. It is necessary, then, to seek a remedy for that situation. The remedy is found. The Pope, whoever he may be, will never come to the secret societies. It is for the secret societies to come first to the Church, in the resolve to conquer the two.

The work which we have undertaken is not the work of a day, nor of a month, nor of a year. It may last many years, a century perhaps, but in our ranks the soldier dies and the fight continues.

We do not mean to win the Popes to our cause, to make them neophytes of our principles, and propagators of our ideas. That would be a ridiculous dream, no matter in what manner events may turn. Should cardinals or prelates, for example, enter, willingly or by surprise, in some manner, into a part of our secrets, it would be by no means a motive to desire their elevation to the See of Peter. That elevation would destroy us. Ambition alone would bring them to apostasy from us. The needs of power would force them to immolate us. That which we ought to demand, that which we should seek and expect, as the Jews expected the Messiah, is a Pope according to our wants. Alexander VI, with all his private crimes, would not suit us, for he never erred in religious matters. Clement XIV, on the contrary, would suit us from head to foot. Borgia was a libertine, a true sensualist of the eighteenth century strayed into the fifteenth. He has been anathematized, notwithstanding his vices, by all the voices of philosophy and incredulity, and he owes that anathema to the vigour with which he defended the Church. Ganganelli gave himself over, bound hand and foot, to the ministers of the Bourbons, who made him afraid, and to the incredulous who celebrated his tolerance, and Ganganelli is become a very great Pope. He is almost in the same condition that it is necessary for us to find another, if that be yet possible. With that we should march more surely to the attack upon the Church than with the pamphlets of our brethren in France, or even with the gold of England. Do you wish to know the reason? It is because by that we should have no more need of the vinegar of Hannibal, no more need the powder of cannon, no more need even of our arms. We have the little finger of the successor of St. Peter engaged in the plot, and that little finger is of more value for our crusade than all the Innocents, the Urbans, and the St. Bernards of Christianity.

We do not doubt that we shall arrive at that supreme term of all our efforts; but when? but how? The unknown does not yet manifest itself. Nevertheless, as nothing should separate us from the plan traced out; as, on the contrary, all things should tend to it, as if success were to crown the work scarcely sketched out tomorrow, we wish in this instruction which must rest a secret for the simple initiated, to give to those of the Supreme-Lodge, councils with which they should enlighten the universality of the brethren, under the form of an instruction or memorandum. It is of special importance, and because of a discretion, the motives of which are transparent, never to permit it to be felt that these counsels are orders emanating from the Alta Vendita. The clergy is put too much in peril by it, that one can at the present hour permit oneself to play with it, as with one of these small affairs or of these little princes upon which one need but blow to cause them to disappear.

Little can be done with those old cardinals or with those prelates, whose character is very decided. It is necessary to leave them as we find them, incorrigible, in the school of Consalvi, and draw from our magazines of popularity or unpopularity the arms which will render useful or ridiculous the power in their hands. A word which one can ably invent and which one has the art to spread amongst certain honourable chosen families by whose means it descends into the cafes, and from the cafes into the streets; a word can sometimes kill a man. If a prelate comes to Rome to exercise some public function from the depths of the provinces, know presently his character, his antecedents, his qualities, his defects above all things. If he is in advance, a declared enemy, an Albani, a Pallotta. a Bernetti, a Della Genga, a Riverola? Envelope him in all the snares which you can place beneath his feet; create for him one of those reputations which will frighten little children and old women; paint him cruel and sanguinary; recount, regarding him, some traits of cruelty which can be easily engraved in the minds of the people. When foreign journals shall gather for us these recitals, which they will embellish in their turn, (inevitably because of their respect for truth) show, or rather cause to be shown, by some respectable fool those papers where the names and the excesses of' the personages implicated are related. As France and England, so Italy will never be wanting in facile pens which know how to employ themselves in these lies so useful to the good cause. With a newspaper, the language of which they do not understand, but in which they will see the name of their delegate or judge, the people have no need of other proofs. They are in the infancy of liberalism; they believe in liberals, as, later on, they will believe in us, not knowing very well why.

Crush the enemy whoever he may be; crush the powerful by means of lies and calumnies; but especially crush him in the egg. It is to the youth we must go, it is that which we must seduce; it is that which we must bring under the banner of the secret societies. In order to advance by steps, calculated but sure, in that perilous way, two things are of the first necessity. You ought have the air of being simple as doves, but you must be prudent as the serpent. Your fathers, your children, your wives themselves, ought always be ignorant of the secret which you carry in your bosoms. If it pleases you, in order the better to deceive the inquisitorial eye, to go often to confession, you are, as by right authorised, to preserve the most absolute silence regarding these things. You know that the least revelation, that the slightest indication escaped from you in the tribunal of penance, or elsewhere, can bring on great calamities, and that the sentence of death is already pronounced upon the revealer, whether voluntary or involuntary.

Now then, in order to secure to us a Pope in the manner required, it is necessary to fashion for that Pope a generation worthy of the reign of which we dream. Leave on one side old age and middle life, go to the youth, and, if possible, even to infancy. Never speak in their presence a word of impiety or impurity, Maxima debetur puero reverentia. Never forget these words of the poet for they will preserve you from licences which it is absolutely essential to guard against for the good of the cause. In order to reap profit at the home of each family, in order to give yourself the right of asylum at the domestic hearth, you ought to present yourself with all the appearance of a man grave and moral. Once your reputation is established in the colleges, in the gymnasiums, in the universities, and in the seminaries-once that you shall have captivated the confidence of professors and students, so act that those who are principally engaged in the ecclesiastical state should love to seek your conversation. Nourish their souls with the splendours of ancient Papal Rome. There is always at the bottom of the Italian heart a regret for Republican Rome. Excite, enkindle those natures so full of warmth and of patriotic fire. Offer them at first, but always in secret, inoffensive books, poetry resplendent with national emphasis; then little by little you will bring your disciples to the degree of cooking desired. When upon all the points of the ecclesiastical state at once, this daily work shall have spread our ideas as the light, then you will be able to appreciate the wisdom of the counsel in which we take the initiative.

Events, which in our opinion, precipitate themselves too rapidly, go necessarily in a few months' time to bring on an intervention of Austria. There are fools who in the lightness of their hearts please themselves in casting others into the midst of perils, and, meanwhile, there are fools who at a given hour drag en even wise men. The revolution which they meditate in Italy will only end in misfortunes and persecutions. Nothing is ripe, neither the men nor the things, and nothing shall be for a long time yet; but from these evils you can easily draw one new chord, and cause it to vibrate in the hearts of the young clergy. That is the hatred of the stranger. Cause the German to become ridiculous and odious even before his foreseen entry. With the idea of the Pontifical supremacy, mix always the old memories of the wars of the priesthood and the Empire. Awaken the smouldering passions of the Guelphs and the Ghibellines, and thus you will obtain for yourselves the reputation of good Catholics and pure patriots.

That reputation will open the way for our doctrines to pass to the bosoms of the young clergy, and go even to the depths of convents.

In a few years the young clergy will have, by the force of events, invaded all the functions. They will govern, administer, and judge. They will form the council of the Sovereign. They will be called upon to choose the Pontiff who will reign; and that Pontiff, like the greater part of his contemporaries, will be necessarily imbued with the Italian and humanitarian principles which we are about to put in circulation. It is a little grain of mustard which we place in the earth, but the sun of justice will develop it even to be a great power; and you will see one day what a rich harvest that little seed will produce.

In the way which we trace for our brethren there are found great obstacles to conquer, difficulties of more than one kind to surmount. They will be overcome by experience and by perspicacity; but the end is beautiful. What does it matter to put all the sails to the wind in order to attain it. You wish to revolutionize Italy? Seek out the Pope of whom we give the portrait. You wish to establish the reign of the elect upon the throne of the prostitute of Babylon? Let the clergy march under your banner in the belief always that they march under the banner of the Apostolic Keys. You wish to cause the last vestige of tyranny and of oppression to disappear? Lay your nets like Simon Barjona. Lay them in the depths of sacristies, seminaries, and convents, rather than in the depths of the sea, and if you will precipitate nothing you will give yourself a draught of fishes more miraculous than his. The fisher of fishes will become a fisher of men. You will bring your-selves as friends around the Apostolic Chair. You will have fished up a Revolution in Tiara and Cope, marching with Cross and banner-a Revolution which it will need but to be spurred on a little to put the four quarters of the world on fire.

Let each act of your life tend then to discover the Philosopher's Stone. The alchemists of the middle ages lost their time and the gold of their dupes in the quest of this dream. That of the secret societies will be accomplished for the most simple of reasons, because it is based on the passions of man. Let us not be discouraged then by a check, a reverse, or a " defeat. Let us prepare our arms in the silence of the lodges, dress our batteries, flatter all passions the most evil and the most generous, and all lead us to think that our plans will succeed one day above even our most improbable calculations.

The Jewish Peril and the Catholic Church

The Catholic Gazette February 1936 Editorial note

That there has been and still is a Jewish problem, no one can deny. Since the rejection of Israel, 1,900 years ago, the Jews have scattered in every direction and in spite of difficulties and even persecution, they have established themselves as a power in nearly every nation of Europe. Jacobs in his <u>Jewish Contributions to Civilization</u>, glories in the fact that without detriment to their own racial unity and international character, the Jews have been able to spread their doctrines and increase their political, social and economic influence among the nations.

In view of this Jewish problem, which affects the Catholic church in a special way, we publish the following amazing extracts from a number of speeches recently made under the auspices of a Jewish society in Paris. The name of our informant must remain concealed. He is personally known to us but by reason of his peculiar relations with the Jews at the present time, we have agreed not todisclose his identity nor to give any further details of the Paris meeting beyond the following extracts which, though sometimes freely translated, nevertheless substantially convey the meaning of the original statements.

****

As long as there remains among the Gentiles any moral conception of the social order, and until all faith, patriotism and dignity are uprooted, our reign of the world shall not come...

We have already fulfilled past of our work, but we cannot yet claim that the whole of our work is done. We have still a long way to gobefore we can overthrow our main opponent: the Catholic Church ...

We must bear in mind that the Catholic Church is the only institution which has stood, and which will, as long as it remains in existence, stand in our way. The Catholic Church, with her methodical work and her edifying and moral teachings, will always keep her children in such a state of mind, as to make them too self-respecting to yield to our domination, and to bow before our future King of Israel ...

That is why we have been striving to discover the best way of shaking the Catholic Church to her very foundations. We have spread the spirit of revolt and false liberalism among the nations of the Gentiles so as to persuade them away from their faith and even to makethem ashamed of professing the precepts of their Religion and boeying the Commandments of their Church. We have brought many of them to boast of being atheists, and more than that, to glory in being descendants of the ape! We have given them new theories, impossible realisation, such as Communism, Anarchism, and Socialism, which are now serving our purpose ... The stupid Gentiles have accepted themwith the greatest enthusiasm, without realising that those theories are ours, and that they constitute our most powerful instrument against themselves ...

We have blackened the Catholic Church with the most ignominious calumnies, we have stained her history and disgraced even her noblest activities. We have imputed to her the wrongs of herenemies, and have thus brought these latter to stand more closely by our side ... So much so, that we are now witnessing, to our great satisfaction, rebellions against the Church in several countries ... We have turned her Clergy into objects of hatred and ridicule, we have subjected them to the contempt of the crowd ... We have caused the practice of the Catholic Religion to be considered out of date and amere waste of time ...

And the Gentiles, in their stupidity, have proved easier dupes than we expected them to be. One would expect more intelligence and more practical common-sense, but they are no better than a herd of sheep Let them graze in our fields till they become fat enough to be immolated to our future King of the World ...

We have founded many secret associations, which all work for our purpose, under our orders and our direction. We have made it an honor, a great honor, for the Gentiles to join us in our organizations, which are, thanks to our gold, flourishing now more than ever. Yet is remains our secret that those Gentiles who betray their own and most precious interests, by joining us in our plot, should never know thatthose associations are of our creation, and that they serve our purpose ...

One of the many triumphs of our Freemasonry is that those Gentiles who become members of our Lodges, should never suspect that we are using them to build their own jails, upon whose terraces we shall erect the throne of our Universal King of Israel; and should never know that we are commanding them to forge the chains of their own servility to our future King of the World.

So far, we have considered our strategy in our attacks upon the Catholic Church from the outside. But this is not all. Let us now explain how we have gone further in our work, to hasten the ruin of the Catholic Church, and how we have penetrated into her most intimate circles, and brought eve some of her Clergy to become pioneers of our cause.

Apart altogether from the influence of our philosophy we have take other steps to secure a breach in the Catholic Church. Let me explain how this has been done.

We have induced some of our children to join the Catholic body, with the explicit intimation that they should work in a still more efficient way for the disintegration of the Catholic Church, by creating scandals within her. We have thus followed the advice of our Prince of the Jews who so widely said: "Let some of your children become canons, so that they may destroy the Church." Unfortunately, not all among the 'convert' Jews have proved faithful to their mission. Many of they have even betrayed us! But, on the other hand, others have kept their promise and honored their word. Thus the counsel of our Elders has proved successful.

We are the Fathers of all Revolutions-even of those which sometimes happen to turn against us. We are the supreme Masters of Peace and War. We can boast of being the Creators of the REFORMATION! Calvin was one of our Children; he was of Jewish descent, and was entrusted by Jewish authority and encouraged withJewish finance to draft his scheme in the Reformation.

Martin Luther yielded to the influence of his Jewish friends, and again, by Jewish authority and with Jewish finance, his plot against the Catholic Church met with success ...

Thanks to our propaganda, to our theories of Liberalism and to our misrepresentations of Freedom, the minds of many among the Gentiles were ready to welcome the Reformation. They separated from the Church to fall into our snare. And thus the Catholic Church has been very sensibly weakened and her authority of the Kings of the Gentiles has been reduced almost to naught ...

We are grateful to Protestants for their loyalty to our wishes-although most of them are, in the sincerity of their faith, unaware of their loyalty to us. We are grateful to them for the wonderful help they are giving us in our fight against the stronghold of Christian Civilization, and in our preparations for the advent of our supremacy over the whole world and over the Kingdoms of the Gentiles.

So far we have succeeded in overthrowing most of the Thrones of Europe. The rest will follow in the near future. Russia has already worshipped our rule. France, with her Masonic Government, is under our thumb. England, in her dependence upon our finance, is under ourheel; and in her Protestantism is our hope for the destruction of the Catholic Church. Spain and Mexico are but toys in our hands. And many other countries, including the U.S.A., have already fallen before our scheming.

But the Catholic Church is still alive ...

We must destroy her without the least delay and without theslightest mercy. Most of the press in the world is under our control; let us therefore encourage in a still more violent way the hatred of the world against the Catholic Church. Let us intensify our activities in poisoning the morality of the Gentiles. Let us spread the spirit of revolution in the minds of the people. They must be made to despise Patriotism and the love of their family, to consider their faith as a humbug, their obedience to the Church as a degrading servility, so that they may become deaf to the appeal of the Church and blind to her warnings against us. Let us, above all, make is impossible for Christians outside the Catholic Church to be reunited with that Church, or for other non-Christians to join that Church; otherwise the greatest obstruction to our domination will be strengthened and all our workundone. Our plot will be unveiled, the Gentiles will turn against us, in the spirit of revenge, and our domination over them will never be realised.

Let us remember that as long as there still remain active enemies of the Catholic Church, we may hope to become Masters of the World ... And let us remember always that the future Jewish King willnever reign in the world before the Pope in Rome is destroyed, as well as all the other reigning Monarchs of the Gentiles upon earth.

Author's Note

Before these facts came to my knowledge, I was rather careless in the fulfillment of my religious duties, but since then,my faith, thank God, has grown stronger and stronger, and my belief in the Catholic Church as being the only bulwark against the nemes of our Christian Civilization, has become firmer than ever. That is why I pray that every Christian be warned against the impending danger of the Jewish plot, so that the whole Christian World may rally under the banner of the Catholic Church, and thus become united against our common, powerful foe.

G.G.

37671966R00020